W9-AHV-206

WHAT DOES A
LINEMAN
DO?

Paul Challen

PowerKiDS press™

New York

Published in 2015 by The Rosen Publishing Group, Inc.
29 East 21st Street, New York, NY 10010

Produced for Rosen by BlueApple*Works* Inc.
Art Director: Tibor Choleva
Designer: Joshua Avramson
Photo Research: Jane Reid
Editor for BlueApple*Works*: Melissa McClellan
US Editor: Joshua Shadowens

Photo Credits: Cover left, p. 7, 20 Susan Leggett/Dreamstime; p. 3 Alhovik/Shutterstock,
background Bruno Ferrari/Shutterstock; p. 4 Dennis Ku/Shutterstock; p. 5, 14, 18 James
Boardman/Dreamstime; p. 6, 9, 11, 12, 14, 19, 21, 23, 29 Andy Cruz; p. 7 Darleen Warnes-
stry/Dreamstime; p. 8 Henrik Lehnerer/Shutterstock; p. 10 Walter Arce/Dreamstime; p.
13, 16 Alexey Stiop/Dreamstime; p. 17 David Park/Dreamstime; p. 22 Olga Bogatyrenko/
Dreamstime; p. 24, 25 bottom Suzanne Tucker/Shutterstock; p. 25 top Todd Taulman/
Dreamstime; p. 26, 27 top Jerry Coli/Dreamstime; p. 27 Molly Williams/Dreamstime; p. 28
Susan Leggett/Shutterstock

Library of Congress Cataloging-in-Publication Data

Challen, Paul C. (Paul Clarence), 1967–
 What does a lineman do? / by Paul Challen.
    pages cm. — (Football smarts)
 Includes index.
 ISBN 978-1-4777-6998-0 (library binding) — ISBN 978-1-4777-6999-7 (pbk.) —
 ISBN 978-1-4777-7000-9 (6-pack)
 1. Line play (Football)—Juvenile literature. 2. Blocking (Football)—Juvenile literature. I.
Title.
 GV951.2.C47 2015
 796.332′26—dc23
                        2014003098

Manufactured in the United States of America

CPSIA Compliance Information: Batch #WS14PK8 For Further Information contact: Rosen Publishing, New York, New York at 1-800-237-9932

TABLE OF CONTENTS

The Football Team 4

Strategy 6

A Lineman's Job 8

The Right Stance 10

The Snap 12

The Center 14

Blocking 16

Solo Blocks 18

Buddy Blocks 20

Pass Protection Blocks 22

The Role of a Coach 24

The Best Linemen 26

Be a Good Sport 28

Glossary 30

For More Information 31

Index 32

THE FOOTBALL TEAM

Football teams have three parts: the **offense**, the **defense**, and special teams. Each part has a different job to do, and so does each player. The offense tries to score points. The defense tries to stop the **opponents** from scoring. Special teams take the field mostly for kicking plays.

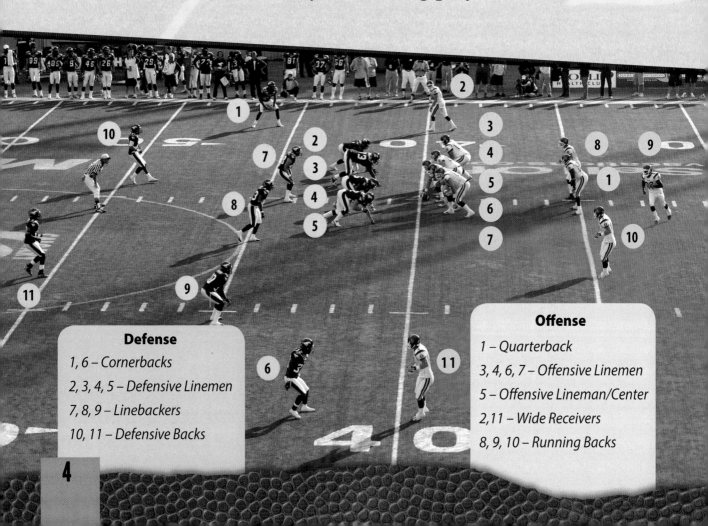

Defense

1, 6 – Cornerbacks

2, 3, 4, 5 – Defensive Linemen

7, 8, 9 – Linebackers

10, 11 – Defensive Backs

Offense

1 – Quarterback

3, 4, 6, 7 – Offensive Linemen

5 – Offensive Lineman/Center

2, 11 – Wide Receivers

8, 9, 10 – Running Backs

Both the offensive and defensive teams include linemen. They are usually the biggest players on a team and spend the most time engaged along the **line of scrimmage**. For most plays, there are five offensive linemen on the field, while the defense has three or four. The offensive linemen team up to open the way for running and passing plays. This is called blocking. Defensive linemen try to stop the offensive blocks.

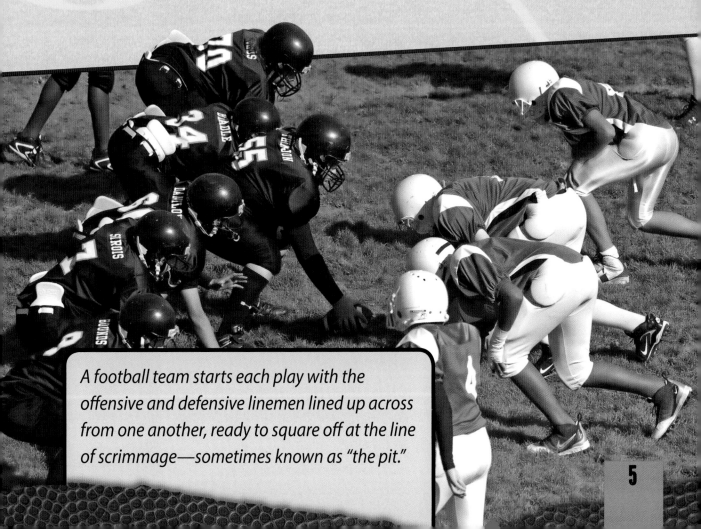

A football team starts each play with the offensive and defensive linemen lined up across from one another, ready to square off at the line of scrimmage—sometimes known as "the pit."

STRATEGY

The offensive line helps the team take the ball down the field toward the opponent's **end zone**. The ball can be advanced by passing it or running with it. The defensive line has an important job to do in trying to stop the offense.

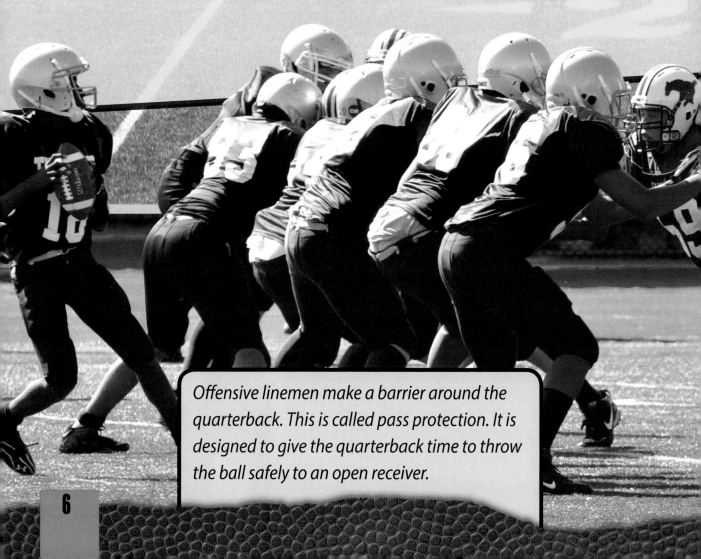

Offensive linemen make a barrier around the quarterback. This is called pass protection. It is designed to give the quarterback time to throw the ball safely to an open receiver.

When a play starts from scrimmage, the offensive and defensive linemen position themselves across from one another. On a passing play, the offensive line works together to protect the **quarterback**, as the defensive linemen try to break through this protection for a **sack**. Linemen must be very strong and physical, but they must be fast on their feet, too. Linemen also need to have a great sense of what is happening all over the field.

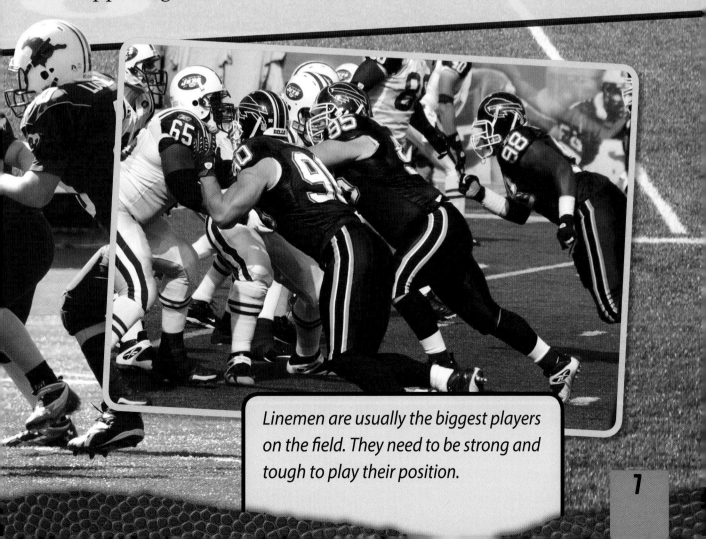

Linemen are usually the biggest players on the field. They need to be strong and tough to play their position.

A LINEMAN'S JOB

There is a lot for a lineman to do on the field. On the snap, he must burst into action and block or rush. The most important job of an offensive lineman is to block his opposing defensive lineman. On passing plays he tries to hold off onrushing tacklers, protecting the quarterback, and giving him time to throw the ball. On running plays, he tries to push the defensive lineman aside, opening up holes for ball carriers to run through.

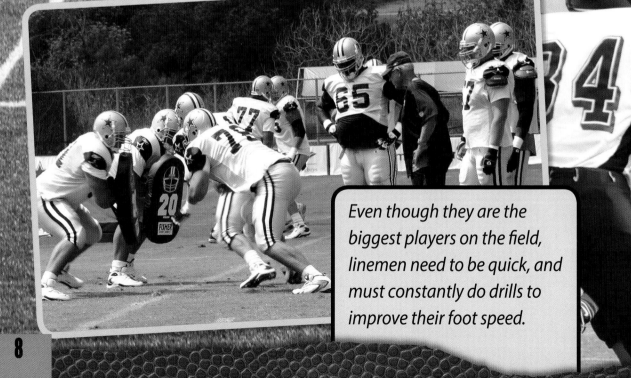

Even though they are the biggest players on the field, linemen need to be quick, and must constantly do drills to improve their foot speed.

Along with the offense and defense, there is another team on the field—the officials! They make sure the rules are followed. The National Football League uses a team of six officials at each game. They are the **referee**, umpire, head linesman, line judge, field judge, and back judge. They have a uniform, too, with black-and-white striped shirts and black or white hats. Sometimes the officials are called "zebras" because of the stripes.

The team that does not have the ball uses a variety of plays on defense. Their goal is to keep the other team from scoring points on offense. The defensive lineman tries to push past the offensive lineman, avoiding blocks. His ultimate goal is to sack the quarterback for a loss of yards, or **tackle** the ball carrier.

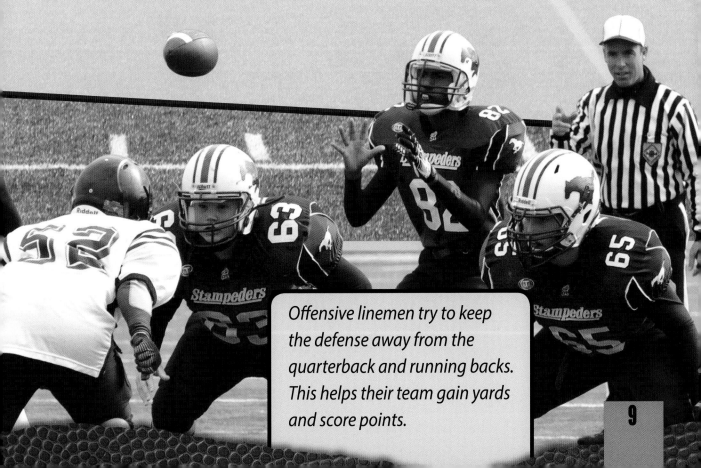

Offensive linemen try to keep the defense away from the quarterback and running backs. This helps their team gain yards and score points.

THE RIGHT STANCE

Offensive and defensive linemen adopt three basic **stances** as they get ready on the line of scrimmage. Offensive linemen can use a two-, three- or four-point stance depending on what play their team uses. Defensive linemen use the three- and four-point stance.

The three-point stance is a great way to explode off the line of scrimmage with balance and power.

In the two-point stance, the offensive lineman gets set in a stand-up crouch with feet about a shoulder's width apart. He puts his hands out front of him, ready to engage his opponent across the line of scrimmage. In the three-point stance, both kinds of lineman crouch down with one hand one the ground, ready to push forward. In the four-point stance, a lineman crouches as in the three-point, but places both hands on the ground.

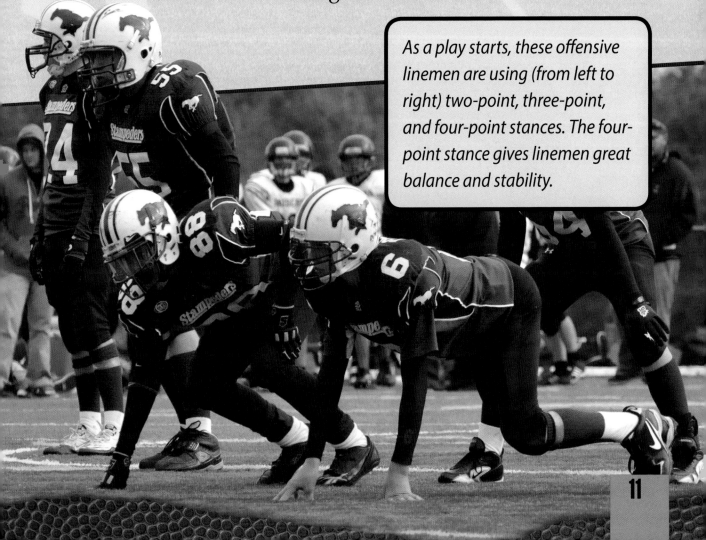

As a play starts, these offensive linemen are using (from left to right) two-point, three-point, and four-point stances. The four-point stance gives linemen great balance and stability.

THE SNAP

For a lineman, the snap that starts each play is extremely important. Offensive linemen know what play their teams will run, and know how the quarterback will "count" the snap—so they have to be ready to react to the quarterback's voice, and must move as a unit to block.

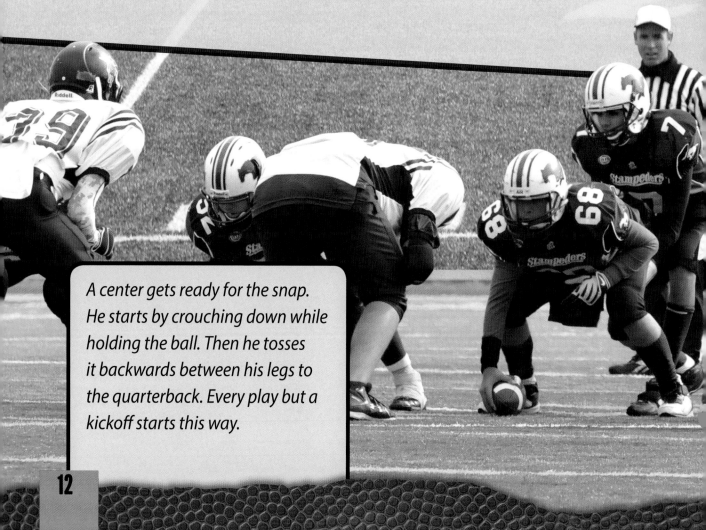

A center gets ready for the snap. He starts by crouching down while holding the ball. Then he tosses it backwards between his legs to the quarterback. Every play but a kickoff starts this way.

Defensive linemen react to the movement of the ball and their opponents across the line. It's illegal for the offensive line to move before the ball is snapped, so the defensive players know they can spring into action as soon as the opponent—just a short distance away—starts moving.

As soon as the ball is snapped, offensive and defensive linemen spring out of their stances and get to work!

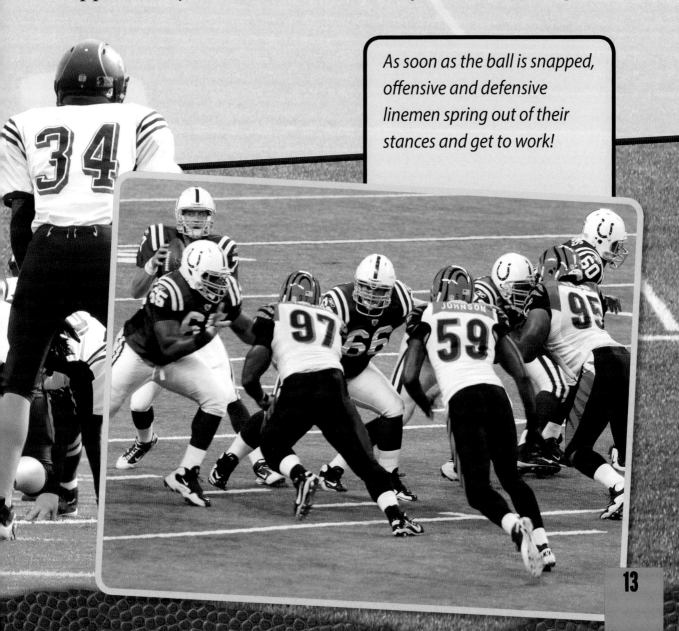

THE CENTER

One of the most important positions on the offensive line is the center. The center is responsible for passing the ball through his legs to the quarterback. The center can execute a direct snap, where he hands the ball directly to the quarterback behind him. He also can do a long (or shotgun) snap, where he passes the ball through his legs and into the air to the quarterback a few yards behind him.

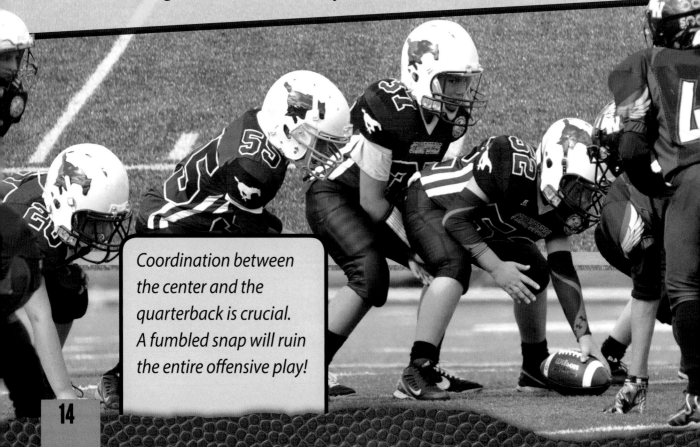

Coordination between the center and the quarterback is crucial. A fumbled snap will ruin the entire offensive play!

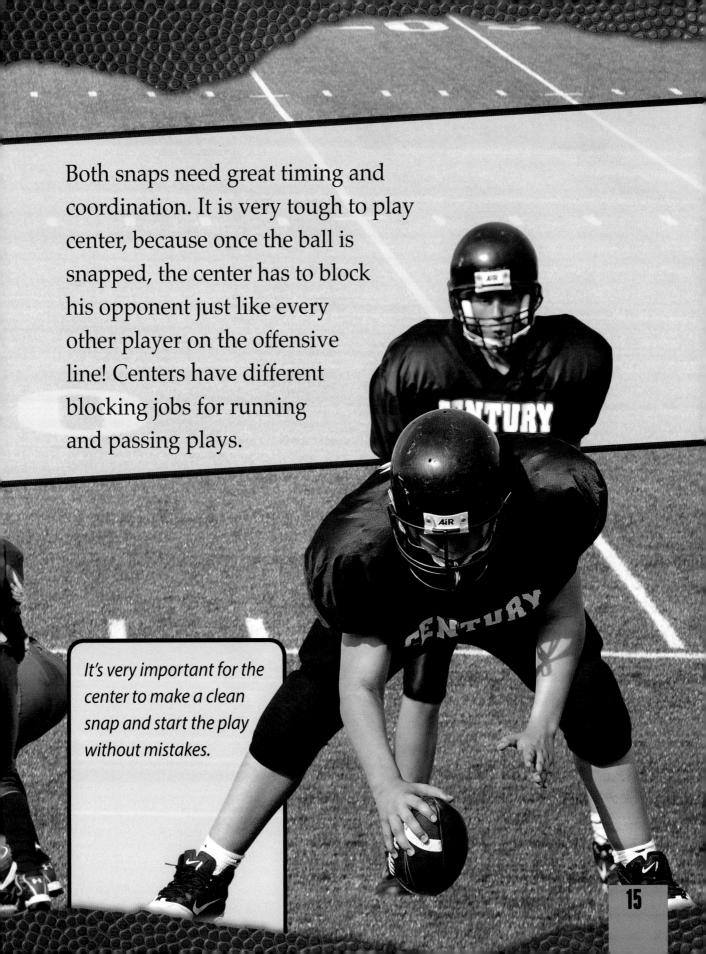

Both snaps need great timing and coordination. It is very tough to play center, because once the ball is snapped, the center has to block his opponent just like every other player on the offensive line! Centers have different blocking jobs for running and passing plays.

It's very important for the center to make a clean snap and start the play without mistakes.

BLOCKING

Blocking may look like simply getting in the way of an opposing player, but it is a very difficult skill to master. **Blockers** must keep their feet moving and hands and arms up to push opponents one way or another. Without good blocking, a team cannot run any offensive play successfully. Of course, defensive players are always looking to get around blocks with every bit of speed and strength they have.

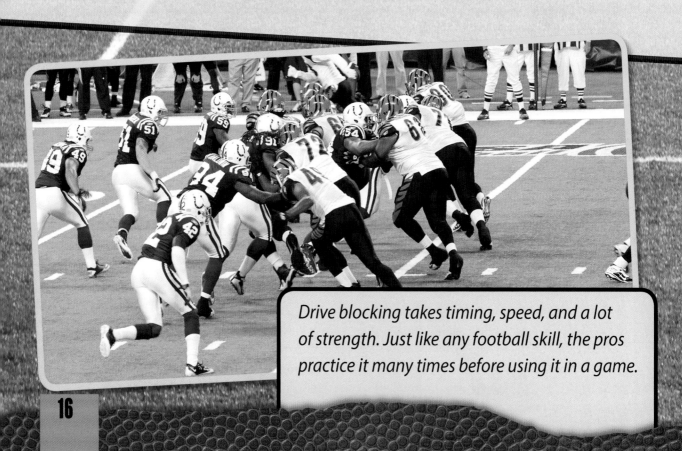

Drive blocking takes timing, speed, and a lot of strength. Just like any football skill, the pros practice it many times before using it in a game.

"Tackle" didn't start as a football word. It comes from a Dutch word, "tacken," which means to grab or hold. By the 18th century, "tackle" had become an English word for equipment used to harness horses. English rugby players began to use "tackle" to describe grabbing or "harnessing" an opponent. Finally the word became an American football term, too.

One of the most common kinds of blocks is the drive block. To execute this one, the offensive lineman takes a short step backwards as soon as the ball is snapped. He then drives forward straight into his opposing lineman, pushing him back. Offensive linemen usually use this block on short-yardage situations.

A drive block is used to force a defensive player off the line of scrimmage as well as tie him up.

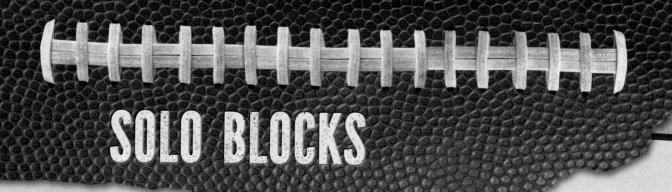

SOLO BLOCKS

A lot of the action on the line of scrimmage is one-on-one blocking, with defensive and offensive linemen battling each other solo. One common solo block is the hook block. In this one, the offensive lineman takes a short step to the side and "hooks" his arm into the chest of the defensive lineman to push him to the side.

Solo blocking is tough because the blocker has to take on the defender one-on-one, with no help from teammates. But if you do it right, it's a great feeling to stop an onrushing lineman.

Another solo block is the angle block. On this one, the defensive lineman moves parallel to the line of scrimmage and angles his body so that his shoulder goes straight into the chest of the defender. It is important for the angle-blocking offensive lineman to understand that the defender will not be focused on him, but will instead be moving toward the offensive player directly in front of him on the line of scrimmage.

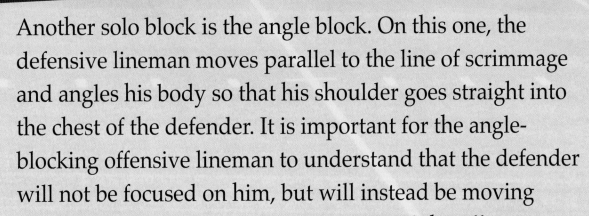

An offensive lineman drives with his legs in order to power a block. He tries to keep his shoulders square and his back straight as he takes short, choppy steps.

BUDDY BLOCKS

An offensive lineman can also work to block in tandem. Known as "buddy blocks," these blocks take communication and teamwork, and are very effective in protecting the quarterback and opening up holes for runners. In a double-team block, one offensive lineman uses an angle block, while his teammate uses a drive block—both against the same opponent.

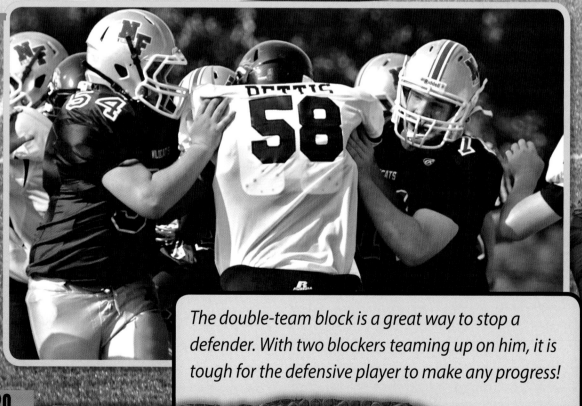

The double-team block is a great way to stop a defender. With two blockers teaming up on him, it is tough for the defensive player to make any progress!

In a combination block, two offensive linemen work together to block two defensive linemen. The aim is to block both defenders in a similar direction as part of a well-planned offensive play. It takes good understanding between blockers to execute a combination block successfully.

A combination block can lead to a fumble by the offense. Though the play may look messy, the defensive linemen did a good job!

PASS PROTECTION BLOCKS

If a quarterback does not have time to look for **receivers**, it is very difficult for any team to run a successful passing play. That's why it is crucial for an offensive lineman to execute pass protection blocks successfully.

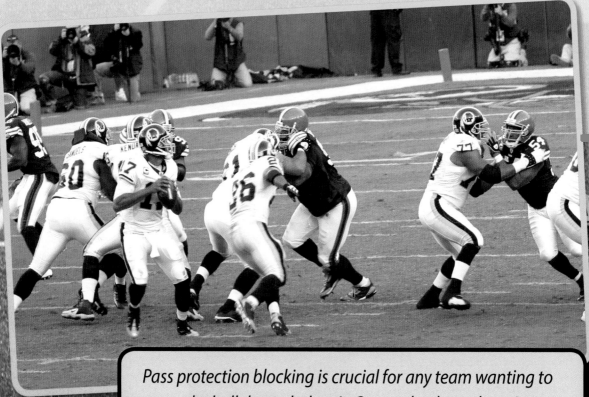

Pass protection blocking is crucial for any team wanting to move the ball through the air. Quarterbacks and receivers often get the credit for a completed pass, but true fans know how important it is for the linemen to do their job!

To do this, he begins in a three-point stance, and then stands up in a crouch when the ball is snapped. Using his arms and hands, he tries to push the onrushing lineman back or to the sides to give his quarterback time to set up and throw. Of course, every defensive lineman looks to get past his opponent on the offensive line to sack the quarterback before he can make a play—so these battles are intense!

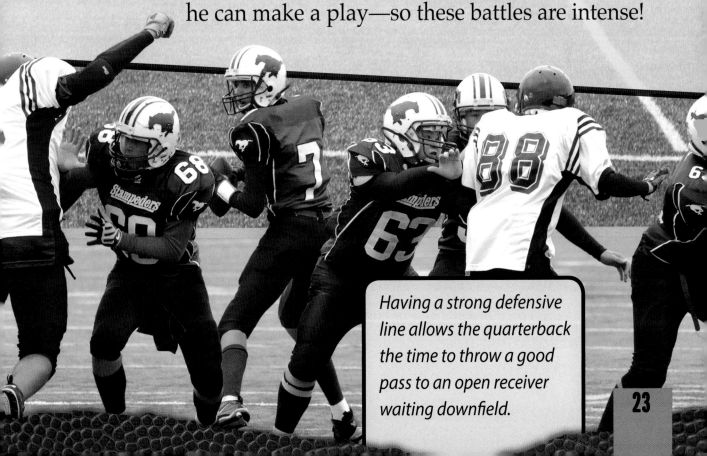

Having a strong defensive line allows the quarterback the time to throw a good pass to an open receiver waiting downfield.

THE ROLE OF A COACH

On a football team, the head coach is responsible for bringing all the parts of the team together. He combines offensive and defensive strategies, and works with players and other coaches to put those plans into action on the field. As well as pre-game planning, the coach also must make important decisions during a game.

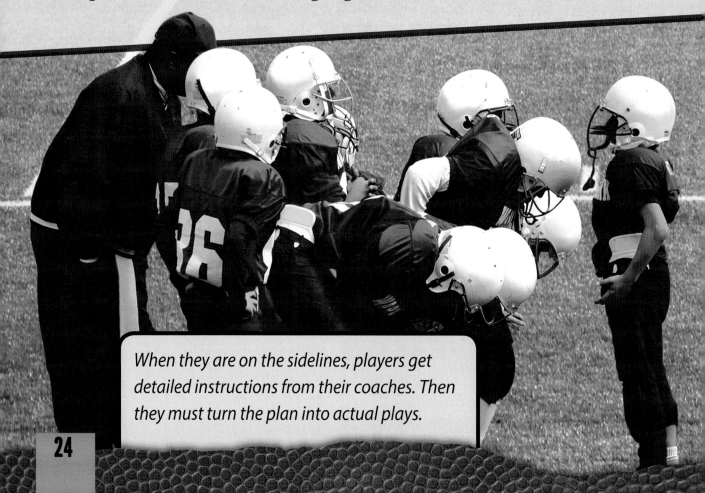

When they are on the sidelines, players get detailed instructions from their coaches. Then they must turn the plan into actual plays.

Coaches are also responsible for the mental side of the game. They must motivate players and make sure everyone is on the same page in understanding a team's goals and how they approach the sport.

Coaches outline the strategies for any given game in a playbook. The offense, defense, and special teams will all have specific playbooks with the complete set of plays that can be called in each situation. A playbook is usually a physical binder given to players when they join a team.

THE BEST LINEMEN

There have been many great linemen—both offensive and defensive—in pro football history. These players have helped their teams win with a combination of speed, strength, and blocking and tackling skills. Superstar defensive linemen have been Randy White of the Dallas Cowboys, Alan Page and Carl Eller of the Minnesota Vikings, and "Mean Joe" Greene of the Pittsburgh Steelers

Howie Long (left) of the Oakland Raiders once made 5 sacks in one game against the Washington Redskins.

Reggie White (right) of the Philadelphia Eagles and Green Bay Packers was picked for an unbelievable 13 Pro Bowls in his 15-year NFL career. He made more than 1,000 tackles and almost 200 sacks as a pro.

Great offensive linemen have included Anthony Muñoz of the Cincinnati Bengals, Orlando Pace of the St. Louis Rams, Art Shell of the Oakland Raiders, Jonathan Ogden of the Baltimore Ravens, Randall McDaniel of the Minnesota Vikings and Tampa Bay Buccaneers, and Mike Webster of the Pittsburgh Steelers.

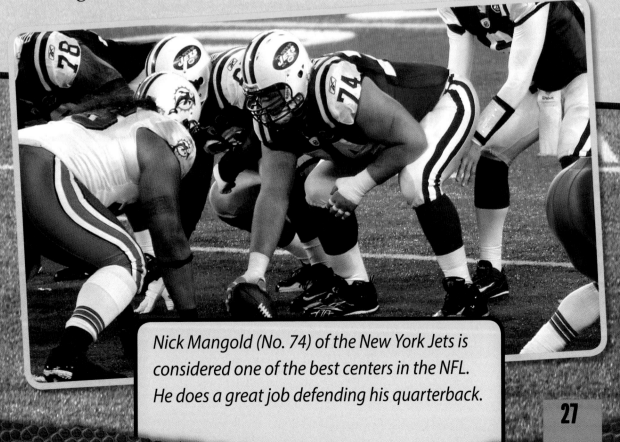

Nick Mangold (No. 74) of the New York Jets is considered one of the best centers in the NFL. He does a great job defending his quarterback.

BE A GOOD SPORT

Even as pro football linemen battle with one another in the heat of a game, they keep in mind that good sportsmanship is a very important part of the game. Of course, it is easy to lose your cool and react in a negative way towards the referees, your opponents, the fans, and even your coach.

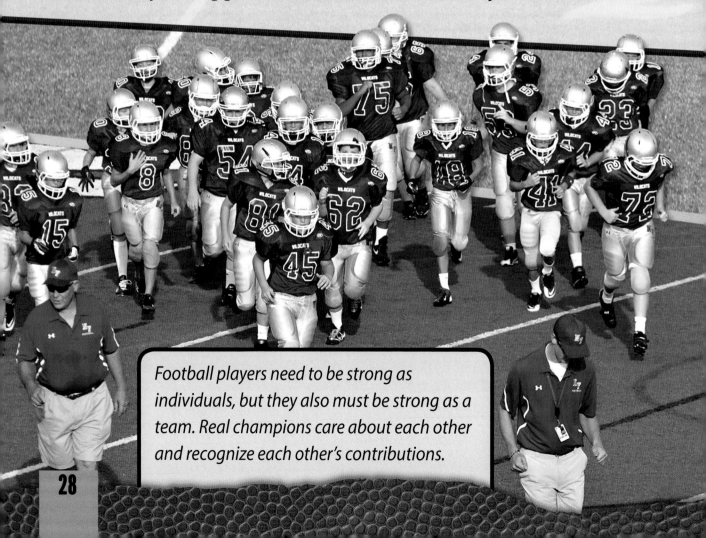

Football players need to be strong as individuals, but they also must be strong as a team. Real champions care about each other and recognize each other's contributions.

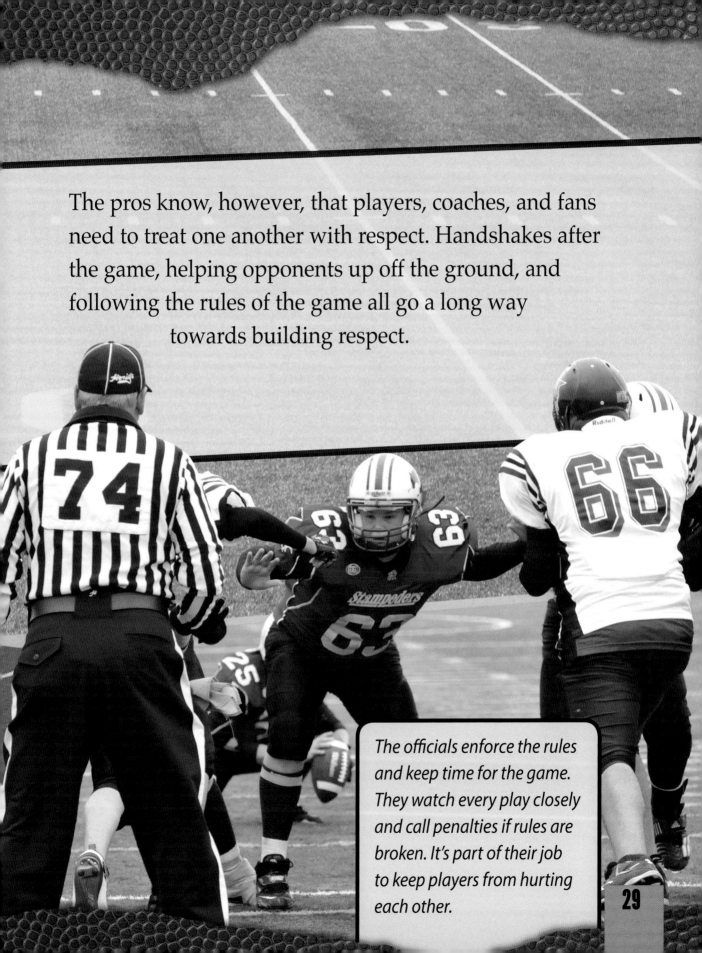

The pros know, however, that players, coaches, and fans need to treat one another with respect. Handshakes after the game, helping opponents up off the ground, and following the rules of the game all go a long way towards building respect.

The officials enforce the rules and keep time for the game. They watch every play closely and call penalties if rules are broken. It's part of their job to keep players from hurting each other.

GLOSSARY

blockers (BLAH-kerz) Players who are trying to stop the other team's players.

defense (DEE-fents) A group of players trying to stop points from being scored by the other team.

end zone (END ZOHN) The area at either end of a football field between the goal line and the end line. A team scores points by getting the ball into the opponents' end zone.

line of scrimmage (LYN UV SKRIH-mij) The invisible line where the ball was last down and where the next play starts.

offense (O-fents) A group of players trying to score points for their team.

opponents (uh-POH-nentz) The people or team you are competing against in a game.

quarterback (KWAHR-ter-bak) The player who lead a team's offense and throws passes to receivers.

receivers (rih-SEE-verz) Offensive players whose main job is to catch passes.

referee (reh-fuh-REE) An official in charge of the game.

sack (SAK) To tackle the quarterback behind the line of scrimmage.

stances (STANS-ez) Ways of standing.

tackle (TA-kul) To knock or throw another player to the ground.

FOR MORE INFORMATION

FURTHER READING

Gifford, Clive. *Football*. Sporting Skills. New York:
Cavendish Square, 2010.

Hoena, Blake A. *Sack Attack!* Sports Illustrated Kids Graphic
Novels. Mankato, MN: Capstone Press, 2012.

McFee, Shane. *Let's Play Football*. Let's Get Active. New York:
PowerKids Press, 2008.

WEBSITES

Due to the changing nature of Internet links, PowerKids Press has
developed an online list of websites related to the subject of this
book. This site is updated regularly. Please use this link to access
the list:

www.powerkidslinks.com/fbs/linem/

INDEX

A

angle block 19, 20

B

blockers 16, 18, 20, 21

buddy blocks 20

C

center 12, 14, 15, 27

coach 24, 25, 28, 29

D

defense 4, 5, 9, 25

defensive linemen 5, 7, 8, 9, 10, 13, 18, 19, 21, 23, 26

drive block 17, 20

E

end zone 6

F

four-point stance 10, 11

fumble 21

L

line of scrimmage 5, 10, 11, 17, 18, 19

O

offense 4, 6, 9, 21, 25

offensive linemen 5, 9, 10, 11, 12, 17, 18, 21, 27

P

pass protection 6, 22

Q

quarterback 6, 7, 8, 9, 12, 14, 20, 22, 23, 27

R

receiver 6, 22, 23

referee 9, 28

S

sack 7, 9, 23, 26, 27

snap 8, 12, 14, 15

solo block 18, 19

special teams 4, 25

sportsmanship 28

stances 10, 11, 13

T

three-point stance 10, 11, 23

two-point stance 11